Church Usher: Servant of God

by

David R. Enlow

Christian Publications

Camp Hill, Pennsylvania

Christian Publications
3825 Hartzdale Drive, Camp Hill, PA 17011

Faithful, biblical publishing—since 1883

ISBN: 0-87509-402-3
LOC Catalog Card Number: 80-66769
© 1982 by Christian Publications
All rights reserved
Printed in the United States of America

97 98 8 7 6 5

Contents

Introduction

"Many pastors are searching for such material to aid their ushers and will benefit from your work," responded Donald Wiggins, pastor of the Westmont Alliance Church, Westmont, Ill. to a survey sent to church leaders seeking help with this manual for ushers.

Several others echoed that view, calling this a "much-needed work," "a most worthwhile project." One pastor said, "We can use all the help you can give us." Thanks in part to these pastors and head ushers, this manual has become a reality.

My own years of service as a church usher, during the pastorate of Dr. A. W. Tozer at Chicago's Southside Christian and Missionary Alliance Church, and later, bring back warm memories. Not only the feeling of satisfaction in serving, but also the rewarding fellowship, stand out in my mind.

In particular, I recall our ushers' banquet one year at a southside restaurant—with wives as guests—featuring special music, inspirational speaker, and pertinent discussions about our duties as ushers. That kind of gathering helps to establish a camaraderie—an *esprit de corps*—worthy of consideration on a regular basis, whether quarterly, semiannually, or once a year.

My special thanks to these men for their invaluable help

in preparation of this manual:

Lucky Baldwin, Wheaton Bible Church, Wheaton, Ill.

Dave Brandon, Fox Valley Bible Church, St. Charles, Ill.

Emil Centanni, Lombard Bible Church, Lombard, Ill.

Dr. Charles A. Epperson, The First Alliance Church, Orlando, Fla.

Rev. Ronald B. Gifford, Blanchard Road Alliance Church, Wheaton, Ill.

Rev. Clarence E. Hager, Lombard Bible Church, Lombard, Ill.

Rev. Stanley J. Lemon, South Holland Alliance Church, South Holland, Ill.

Carl Lofgren, Wheaton Bible Church, Wheaton, Ill.

Ed Mark, South Holland Alliance Church, South Holland, Ill.

Oscar McCullough, Moody Church, Chicago, Ill.

Ray Munsterman, Blanchard Road Alliance Church, Wheaton, Ill.

David Riemenschneider, Bloomingdale Alliance Church, Bloomingdale, Ill.

Dean Sonntag, Westmont Alliance Church, Westmont, Ill.

Rev. Howard C. Stein, Fox Valley Bible Church, St. Charles, Ill.

Rev. Donald A. Wiggins, Westmont Alliance Church, Westmont, Ill.

Flexibility is a key consideration as you read this manual and seek to apply its principles and suggestions to your own church situation. You must adapt the ideas presented, depending on the size of your fellowship, its flavor (formal or informal) and other factors. This book contains suggestions, not directions.

One church surveyed, for example, likes military precision in the performance of usher duties; another leans toward informality. Who is to say one is right and the other is wrong? Another key word is *balance*. By not going overboard in any particular area, a church maintains a worshipful atmosphere and the ushers are instrumental in that achievement.

Hopefully, this manual will provide a basis for study and training among your church ushers. At the very least, it should remind your ushers that theirs is a vital spiritual ministry.

In addition to the pastors and head ushers who contributed their expertise to this manual, I am indebted to these three sources for helpful information:

Paul H. D. Lang. *Church Ushering*. St. Louis: Concordia Publishing House, 1946.

Willis O. Garrett. *Church Usher's Manual*. Old Tappan: Fleming H. Revell, 1924.

Leslie Parrott. *The Usher's Manual*. Grand Rapids: Zondervan Publishing House, 1970.

1

The Ministry of Ushering

Four great ministries comprise the work of the church: preaching, teaching, music, and ushering. Each one is vital to the spiritual success of the church, for without any one of them the total ministry will suffer.

First and foremost, the church usher is a servant. Too, he is one who exercises his spiritual gift, for the ministry of ushering surely must be included in the gift of helps referred to by the Apostle Paul in his letter to the Corinthians:

> And God hath set some in the church, first apostles, secondarily prophets, thirdly teachers, after that miracles, then gifts of healings, helps, governments, diversities of tongues (1 Cor. 12:28).

In his role as a servant, the usher is reminded: "...by love *serve* one another" (Gal. 5:13). "...if any man *serve* me, him will my Father honour" (John 12:26).

The faithful church usher finds his motto in Colossians 3:23, 24: "And whatever ye do, do it heartily, as to the Lord, and not unto men, Knowing that of the Lord ye shall receive the reward of the inheritance: for ye serve the Lord Christ." The usher should constantly remind himself: "*I serve the Lord Christ.*" That will add a whole new spiritual dimension to his service.

Like all true believers who remain stedfast in their service for the Lord, the church usher stands to hear those glorious words some day: "Well done, thou good and faithful servant; thou hast been faithful over a few things, I will make thee ruler over many things: enter thou into the joy of thy lord" (Matt. 25:21).

This idea of service is kept constantly before the ushers and the congregation of the Lombard Bible Church. Pastor Clarence E. Hager frequently introduces the offering with these remarks: "As the ushers come forward, I want to remind you that as they serve us, they are serving the Lord."

Pastor Howard C. Stein of the Fox Valley Bible Church, echoed the view of others: "The ministry of ushering creates an atmosphere; it sets a tempo for the service to follow. It is a part of the worship service."

Most pastors agree that church ushering itself is an act of worship. The usher is responsible for maintaining an atmosphere of reverence and order before, during, and after the service. His attitude is influenced greatly by such scriptural admonitions as these:

"But the Lord is in his holy temple: let all the earth keep silence before him" (Hab. 2:20).

"God is greatly to be feared in the assembly of the saints, and to be had in reverence of all them that are about him" (Ps. 89:7).

As host for God Himself, the church usher should help people feel comfortable and at home. "Come unto me, all ye that labour and are heavy laden, and I will give you rest" (Matt. 11:28).

In the words of Pastor Donald Wiggins, Westmont Alliance Church, "An usher can serve as a representative for Christ, either drawing people to Him or driving them away."

Dean Sonntag, head usher at the Westmont church, considers his role a very important function. "In many cases," he said, "the first impressions visitors to the church experience are those of the ushers."

Ushering, in the Old Testament, is perhaps best exemplified by Psalms 84:10, ". . .I had rather be a *doorkeeper* [italics added] in the house of my God, than to dwell in the tents of wickedness."

In the New Testament, it seems clear that Jesus often used His disciples as ushers:

> And he commanded the multitude to sit down on the ground. And he took the seven loaves and the fishes, and gave thanks, and brake them, and gave to his disciples, and the disciples to the multitude. And they did all eat, and were filled: and they took up of the broken meat that was left seven baskets full (Matt. 15:35-37).

Pastor Ronald B. Gifford of the Blanchard Road Alliance Church, declared that "a smooth service happens only when ushers are faithful. Their greeting of people—especially guests—is seriously undervalued."

His head usher, Ray Munsterman, emphasized one of the prime functions of the usher: "Visitors should be welcomed warmly and made to feel at home."

Ed J. Mark, South Holland Alliance Church, stressed the

point that church ushers "should have pride in their work and perform their duties as unto the Lord."

Other scriptural injunctions seem to apply directly to the church usher, or to the ministry of ushering itself. "Let all things be done decently and in order" (I Cor. 14:40).

It is largely up to the church usher to see that this command is obeyed.

"Ye are the salt of the earth. . ." (Matt. 5:13). To a great extent, the usher is responsible for the "flavor" of a service.

"Let your speech be always with grace, seasoned with salt. . ." (Col. 4:6). Self-control in use of the tongue is especially important to the church usher, for he often is the only contact a person may have with the church.

"Let your light so shine before men, that they may see your good works, and glorify your Father which is in heaven" (Matt. 5:16). As the first official representative of Jesus Christ seen by most visitors, the usher's light must burn brightly, which of course means that the fruit of the Spirit must be very evident in his life.

> But the fruit of the Spirit is love, joy, peace, longsuffering, gentleness, goodness, faith, meekness, temperance: self-control. . . (Gal. 5:22, 23).

Christ's *love* must radiate in and through the usher. Then it will be obvious to member and visitor alike that the love of God is alive and well in the church usher who serves Him.

Since the scriptural promise is true, ". . .in thy presence is fullness of joy. . ." (Ps. 16:11), the effective church usher should show forth that *joy* in the performance of his duties.

11

He has the priceless privilege of setting the tone for the service.

Part of that "tone" is a sense of *peace* that should pervade the atmosphere, and the Spirit-filled and Spirit-led usher—who has yielded himself to the Holy Spirit anew as he begins his duties—is one who manifests that peace in his own spirit and manner.

When overflow crowds or unexpected disturbances make the usher's job more demanding, it is then that *long-suffering*—or patience—becomes a most desirable trait.

Gentleness is a virtue that makes strong men even stronger. In every situation, the Spirit-filled usher responds by being gentle, no matter what the provocation might be.

A good man, in scriptural terms, is one who obviously and demonstrably reflects honor and glory to his Lord. Surely that trait of *goodness* should characterize the church usher. In reality, that goodness is the righteousness of God imparted to the believer.

Meekness—"power under control," as Dr. Warren Wiersbe once defined it—denotes a humble spirit that befits the servant role of the usher. It reminds the usher that he is there to serve, not to boss.

Faith—or *faithfulness*, as the Living Bible translates the word—refers to one of the most important qualities any servant of God possesses. Without dependability, the church usher is lacking a vital characteristic.

Self-control is perhaps best described in Proverbs 16:32, "He that is slow to anger is better than the mighty; and he that ruleth his spirit than he that taketh a city." By the very nature of his position, the usher has little problem being "slow to anger," but it is not always easy to rule one's spirit when circumstances dictate otherwise.

The church usher has a unique opportunity to display the grace of Christ by his attitude and the atmosphere he creates.

"Ushering sets a tone—hopefully one of friendliness, concern, helpfulness—for visitors," observed David E. Brandon, Fox Valley Bible Church.

David Riemenschneider, Bloomingdale Alliance Church, pointed out that church ushering done right is an evidence of a well-organized church, and certainly the visitor has a right to expect that when he appears for worship.

Rev. Stanley J. Lemon, South Holland Alliance Church, reinforced this view. "The initial impression of visitors is communicated through the greeting given by the ushers."

Other Scriptures point forcefully to the type of servant-hood that belongs to the church usher. ". . .Do good unto all men, especially unto them who are of the household of faith" (Gal. 6:10). "Study to show thyself approved unto God, a workman that needeth not to be ashamed. . ." (2 Tim. 2:15).

In the matter of taking his work—not himself—seriously, the usher has the example of Jesus in Matthew 11:29, ". . . learn of me; for I am meek and lowly of heart. . . ."

In his very helpful *The Usher's Manual*, Leslie Parrott suggests an usher's prayer that might well be uttered just prior to his servant's role at each service:

May I, dear Lord, in church today, fulfill my assignment in a Christ-like way. Make me efficient in what I do, effective in what I say, under-

13

standing by the way I feel about people, and helpful in the attitudes I have toward them.

Make me a co-worker with the pastor, the church musicians, the teachers, and most of all, Lord, with Thee.

Save me from hurtful words and harmful deeds. Make people glad they came to our church today because the Holy Spirit ministered to their needs through the sermon and prayer of the pastor, through the music of the organist and singers, through the explanations of understanding teachers, and through the ministry of ushers like me.

In Christ's Name, Amen.[1]

To add even greater significance to the role of usher, Parrot also recommends a special usher's commission, to be read publicly to the church ushers at the beginning of their term of service each year:

At the beginning of another year, the church gives you this fresh commission, new and yet old. Allow the hospitality of this church to become incarnate in you.

Wrap every word and clothe every action in the spirit of human kindness. May your kind of Christianity help people to let down their guards, open their hearts and relax their minds for the worship of God and direction of His Holy Spirit.

Be understanding with the difficult person. Exercise compassion with all kinds of people.

Learn to be efficient, but not at the expense of kindness. And accept from the pastor and congregation this assignment which ranks in importance with the other ministries of this church.

May your highest good be the kindness of human understanding, your greatest virtue the stability of a man in Christ, and your most effective tool the indwelling presence of the Holy Spirit who is the Spirit of Christ.[2]

Summary:

1.   Four great church ministries: preaching, teaching, music, and ushering.

2.   The church usher is a *servant*, exercising the gift of *helps*.

3.   Church ushering itself is an act of worship.

4.   As *salt* and *light*, the usher should demonstrate the fruit of the Spirit.

5.   The church usher should take his work—never himself—seriously.

1. Leslie, Parrott, *The Usher's Manual*. Grand Rapids: Zondervan Publishing House, 1970, p. 22.
2. Ibid.

The Usher's Importance in the Total Church Program

If the role of the church usher is one of ministry, which seems obvious in the light of appropriate Scriptures on the subject, then it is an important responsibility that bears on the life and program of the church as a whole.

In a very real way, church ushering bears significantly on every aspect of the ministry of the church. Evangelistically, for example, the usher has a dual role.

First and foremost, he himself is a witness—an evangelist. As such, he must be especially sensitive and alert to every opportunity to represent Jesus Christ to visitors of the church, many of whom might be there without saving faith.

Secondly, as a representative of (1) God, (2) pastor, (3) church, and (4) members, the church usher automatically becomes an example of the believer to those who visit the church and may not have any kind of contact with persons other than the usher. With that awesome responsibility in mind, the usher must prepare himself for his vital role in the same way the pastor has to gird himself spiritually for his public ministry.

How does the usher accomplish this important task of preparation? Primarily, it seems, a spiritual inventory is necessary that will cleanse the wrong and accentuate the right—a "getting right with God" that includes restoring any broken relationships that might exist on a horizontal plane—person to person.

"If I regard iniquity in my heart, the Lord will not hear me" (Ps. 66:18). Whatever wrong feeling may have crept in toward a fellow human being—whether believer or unbeliever—must be dealt with, and there is a way out of the difficulty.

"If we confess our sins, he is faithful and just to forgive us our sins, and to cleanse us from all unrighteousness" (I John 1:9). On the horizontal level, the way is made equally plain.

"Confess your faults one to another, and pray one for another, that ye may be healed. The effectual fervent prayer of a righteous man availeth much" (James 5:16).

Just as church ushering may rightly be considered an evangelistic arm of the church, so might it be thought of as a public relations agency.

What people in general, and visitors in particular, think of your church will depend in a great measure on their initial reaction to their first visit. And more often than not, their only contact on that occasion was with an usher— who thus became an important spokesman and representative for the church.

Any church activity that bears so heavily on evangelistic outreach and dispensing good will must be considered vital in the total church program. Most church leaders concur with that view.

"The ushers put a warm face on the entire church," declared Rev. Ronald B. Gifford, "especially for new people. They help people relax when they appear confident and friendly, and when they work smoothly."

"Keeping the doors closed and late-comers out at critical times early in the service is a hard responsibility," he added, "but if they don't, the concentration of all others is damaged."

Dr. Charles A. Epperson, the First Alliance Church, Orlando, Fla., described ushers as "vital to every facet of the work. Much of the worship atmosphere is related to the functioning of the ushers."

In a similar vein, Rev. Clarence E. Hager observed that "careful, friendly seating of people encourages proper worship."

Rev. Howard C. Stein stressed that "the usher is the church extended, the church on display, as far as image, personality, attitude, and even commitment are concerned. Their ministry can be supportive, or it can be disruptive."

Efficient flow of people into the service lends a "personal touch to the church," in the view of David Riemenschneider. "A disorganized effort is a distraction," he added.

Rev. Donald A. Wiggins observed: "The ushers facilitate smooth and orderly worship. They also serve as 'forerunners' for our ministries by giving a genuinely friendly reception.

"I depend on the ushers to respond quickly to noise disturbances," he said, "and to any special instructions from the pulpit. I also want them to seat late-comers in a way that will cause the least distraction to others."

Dean Sonntag agreed that "good ushering results in a smooth service. When this takes place, the congregation can experience true worship with no distractions.

"When the ushers perform well," he added, "their actions

are noticed by the congregation."

Dave Brandon declared that "the usher is an important part of the worship hour. Usher performance should project friendliness and warmth."

While his role and responsibility seem relatively unimportant, the church usher in reality is of prime importance in the overall ministry of the church. Good ushering promotes good services and helps people experience worship.

That, perhaps, accounts for the fact that an increasing number of churches delegate responsibility for usher supervision and support to the worship committee of the church.

One head usher, Ed Mark, observed that "pastors appreciate a well-organized ushering staff"—an understatement, to be sure, in the light of pastoral response to the subject.

Ray Munsterman declared: "Ushers can make visitors feel welcome, thereby helping to give people a desire to return, thus causing the church to grow."

One pastor confessed that the role of the usher "has not been considered in a significant manner in relation to the total church ministry. It is a role that has been assumed without extensive thought." And his honest expression no doubt reflects the situation that is prevalent in many churches today.

But that pastor, and many others, seem willing to consider the subject further—on a more serious level—with a new realization of the total impact made by an effective usher on the overall program of the church.

If the role of the usher is indeed so important, what efforts have been made to establish and maintain *esprit*

19

de corps among these choice servants of the church?

The Wheaton Bible Church, under the capable leadership of usher committee co-chairmen Lucky Baldwin and Carl Lofgren, have several ways of accomplishing that worthy goal.

Members of their ushering staff keep in close contact with each other, remembering birthdays, anniversaries, and other significant observances of their co-laborers. They show and express personal concern for each other.

Their annual Christmas dinner, with their wives, features food, fun, and games, along with singing and a brief devotional message. A wholesome camaraderie exists among the ushers.

Similarly, Dr. Charles A. Epperson reports that his church sponsors an annual covered dish supper for ushers and their wives. To further maintain *esprit de corps* among the ushers, the pastor frequently offers words of public commendation and from time to time expresses his appreciation personally to his ushers.

No effort will be made in this manual to deal at length with the subject of women ushers. Suffice it to say that at least one of the churches surveyed does make use of women ushers, a practice begun primarily because of a need for additional volunteers that was not met by the men.

One head usher expressed the view that in his church neither the women nor the men favored the idea of having ushers of both sexes. In the one church surveyed that is now known to have both men and women in that role, the practice has continued for many months with good success.

Another pastor who likes to bolster usher morale is Rev. Clarence E. Hager, who also employs personal compli-

20

ments and public recognition to accomplish that end.

Emil Centanni, of the Lombard Bible Church, feels that prayer is essential in maintaining close fellowship among the ushers. "I keep them on my prayer list," he said, "and try to talk with them whenever I can."

At the Fox Valley Bible Church in St. Charles, Ill., "*esprit de corps* among our ushers is encouraged by example and by recognition, and by a positive, forward attitude at all times," Rev. Howard C. Stein declared.

The two considerations go hand in hand: if church ushering is vital to the total program of the church, which indeed it is, then it is vitally important to recognize their key contribution in whatever ways present themselves.

Summary:

1. Church ushering is an evangelistic arm of the church.

2. Church ushering is a public relations agency of the church.

3. Therefore, it is important that the usher maintain a close spiritual relationship with the Lord and with his fellow human beings.

4. The ushers facilitate smooth and orderly worship.

5. Special effort should be made to establish and maintain *esprit de corps* among the ushers.

3

What Does an Usher Need to Know about the Church?

To properly fulfill his duties and responsibilities, the church usher must be one of the best-informed people in the congregation. As Carl Lofgren suggested, he should know as much as possible about the church.

Adding to that view, Dr. Charles A. Epperson said: "He should be thoroughly knowledgeable of the entire facility and where each group meets. He should know enough about the church doctrinally and administratively to answer the 'chance' question that may be asked by a visitor."

Church office hours should be familiar to the usher. Some visitor might want an appointment with the pastor, and immediate availability of the necessary information would be most helpful.

If the church operates a bus or buses, the exact schedules should be known. This might involve students and/or children, and the information should be kept in mind at all times as data vital to the welfare of some members and guests.

The usher should be able to give clear and concise restroom locations.

Even information as to the pastor's educational and professional background might come in handy for the occasional visitor—and the well-informed usher makes a good impression for the church.

Some visitor, too, might ask something about a *church manual or book of discipline*. To have such information immediately available is going the "second mile" insofar as the visitor is concerned, but is certainly a worthwhile effort.

Knowing one's denominational headquarters location might seem like excess data, but again it displays a wealth of knowledge that can only impress the visitor and convince him that someone really cares—to go to that extent of storing up information for questions that might arise.

Large churches, in particular, have parking facilities that should be known clearly by the usher, so that he can give proper instructions to inquirers.

Even such seemingly inconsequential information as the denominational publishing house location might well be helpful to visitors at one time or another.

At the very least, ushers should know where every Sunday school department and class meets, for this information is vital especially to visitors with children.

Similarly, the usher should know where nursery facilities are and what policies govern them.

Every usher would do well to familarize himself with the location of heating, plumbing, and electrical controls. Such knowledge might well forestall potential emergencies that could endanger the lives of worshippers.

Such a mundane matter as telephones and policy as to their use is another bit of information that should be known by the ushers. In cases of emergency, particularly, such information would be vital.

Lost and found objects might be a source of concern for some guests or members who have misplaced prized items. One central place for holding all such items is ideal, and objects discovered by the ushers in various parts of the church should be taken to the one central place.

Where is first aid material in your church? Surely the usher must have this information available at all times, for the obvious reason that emergencies—minor or major—might demand the use of such material on a moment's notice.

Ed Mark added two further informational concerns for the usher: "coat racks and time and place for all meetings of the church." While most bulletins give the latter information, it is still wise to have such information stored up in one's mind for immediate access.

Rev. Stanley J. Lemon added: "Literature available on the denomination; church assistance ministries; junior church."

Ray Munsterman suggested that "the more the church usher knows, the more effectively he can do his job."

Rev. Howard C. Stein painted a broader picture: "The ushers should be thoroughly knowledgeable—thrust, purposes and desires of the church."

Rev. Donald Wiggins summarized his views: "The usher needs to be fully informed as to location of all facilities and rooms, the schedule of services and activities, and to whom he should refer specific questions outside of his responsibility."

In a similar vein, Rev. Clarence E. Hager said: "He must be thoroughly acquainted with all its facilities—nursery, restrooms, water fountains, exits, junior church arrangements and location."

Rev. Ronald B. Gifford felt it was especially important that the church usher "needs to be able to direct new people to classes."

In short, the usher must be well-informed. He should know all the buildings and programs. He should know the key persons in each ministry of the church. A working knowledge of the church enables him to serve effectively.

Even such a simple matter as knowing where to find a glass or paper cup sometimes is instrumental in helping to solve an immediate problem; e.g., the pastor developing a "frog in his throat" and needing a few swallows of water to restore his voice to normalcy.

And if the storing up of pertinent information is vital to the usher's efficiency, what is being done to facilitate such learning and to encourage the ushers to increase their church knowledge on a continuing basis?

Of the churches surveyed, a surprising number confessed that nothing much is being done along these lines. However, most of these vowed to begin such a program right away that would keep their ushers well-informed on a continuing basis.

One pastor expressed the views of several others as well when he said that "plans are being made to have regular meetings with the ushers to aid in communication."

How does a huge church like Wheaton Bible Church handle this particular problem? Co-chairmen Carl Lofgren and Lucky Baldwin not only operate on a person-to-person basis with their ushers, but they also meet briefly before each service to share pertinent information and on occasion, when major changes are involved, they hold special meetings—perhaps on a Sunday afternoon—to update their entire ushering staff.

Whatever method is used—person-to-person, brief pre-service meetings or special group sessions—the important thing is to see that lack of communication does not hinder the smooth-working operations of the ushers and thus in any way mar the service.

Summary:

1. The usher should be thoroughly knowledgeable about the church—its programs, personnel, and facilities.

2. Specifically, it would be helpful to know about church office hours, bus schedules, restroom locations, pastor's educational and professional background, church manual or book of discipline, denominational headquarters and publishing house locations, parking facilities, Sunday school department and classrooms, nursery, heating, plumbing and electrical controls, telephones, lost and found, first aid, coat racks, time and place for all meetings, denominational literature, exits, junior church.

3. Dissemination of such information on a continuing basis is vitally important and may be maintained in several different ways: person-to-person, pre-service briefings, group meetings perhaps on a Sunday afternoon from time to time, when needed.

4

The Organization of the Ushers

Ultimate authority for the supervision of the church ushers rests in the hands of the pastor, but usually he is glad to delegate this responsibility on a week-to-week basis to one of the official boards of the church.

Each church organizes its ushers to meet its own need, but good organization is essential if the work is to be accomplished.

Elements of organization to be considered include the following: a chairman or head usher to coordinate activities; a system of team selection and rotation; reporting system; recruiting and training of new ushers.

At the Westmont Alliance Church, according to Pastor Donald Wiggins, "the head usher is selected by the deacons and approved by the executive committee. He in turn selects the other ushers. Usher matters are discussed in deacon meetings."

Head usher Dean Sonntag, of the same church, adds: "The head usher makes assignments on a monthly basis. We also have an assistant head usher. Our six ushers for the Sunday morning service are on duty four consecutive weeks. Since eighteen ushers are available, this means that each man serves only one month out of the quarter."

Oscar McCullough, Moody Church, Chicago, reports that his church has an usher director, an assistant director, four section heads, fifty-five regular ushers and twenty-five substitutes.

Wheaton Bible Church, on the other hand, has two co-chairmen, eight head ushers (two for each main service) and a growing list of active, reserve, and prospective ushers. The co-chairmen are authorized to select their ushers. These two leaders of the ushering staff report to the chairman of the Worship Department.

At the First Alliance Church in Orlando, Fla., the ushers are responsible to the Board of Deacons. The deacons select the new ushers at the first organizational meeting of each year.

Rev. Stanley J. Lemon reports that the South Holland Alliance Church elects two ushers at each annual meeting, to serve only for one year at a time, and they are directly responsible to the pastor.

Ed Mark elaborates: "The nominating committee submits names, and there is no limit on the number of consecutive terms of service to which they may be elected."

Fox Valley Bible Church organizes its ushers through the Fellowship Department. "It is a part of the worship experience," Pastor Howard C. Stein declared. "Ushers serve from two to four Sundays a month. Each service has four ushers.

"The ushers are selected by the chairman of the Fellowship Department or by a key usher he has selected—on the basis of friendliness, warmth of personality, ability, appearance, and commitment to Christ."

Dave Brandon, of the same church, adds: "Hopefully, the

usher team is comprised of one or two experienced members and two or three who are relatively new to the church—thus bringing them into closer relationship with the church.

"We have a pool of about twenty ushers. Though we have no formal meetings, the head usher is kept apprised of needs."

Rev. Ronald B. Gifford reports that "the head usher selects the team for each service, with one person in charge of each team. They are responsible to the chairman of the Worship Committee.

"Though we have no training program, I give them a job description and also specific written instructions each week."

Ray Munsterman adds: "We have four ushers each for the two morning services and the evening service, and the areas of service are rotated for a change of pace.

"Occasionally we are able to alternate so that the ushers serve every other Sunday. Our ushers are trained on the job."

David Riemenschneider, pastor of the smaller Bloomingdale Alliance Church, reports that his ushers are deacons. "The head usher serves every week; the others, twice a month. They meet once a month (as deacons), and of course are responsible to the chairman of the Board of Deacons."

At the Lombard Bible Church, according to Pastor Clarence E. Hager, "The Committee on Standing Committees, appointed by the Executive Board, nominates to elect ushers. This manual will help in their training."

Wheaton Bible Church, like many others, has found that on-the-job training is quite satisfactory. Co-chairmen

Baldwin and Lofgren try to place new ushers alongside the more experienced to facilitate such training.

For the benefit of its very effective usher program, this church has several helpful forms. One is the "Public Service Format," with blanks at the top for "Day, Date, Time" and columns headed: "Time," "Program Item," "Personality," "Sound," "Lights," and "Music." A detailed schedule is filled out for each service, and copies go to each usher involved.

Another form is "Greeter and Head Usher Schedule" for one quarter at a time. For each service, two head ushers and three greeters are listed, with phone numbers for the head ushers and exact assignments (i.e., "East Door") for the greeters.

Their special note on this form is quite instructive:

> Greeters for the 9:30 a.m. service should be at the doors by 9:10 a.m. and remain until the offering has been taken; for the 11:00 a.m. service by 10:30 a.m. and remain until the offering has been taken; and for the 6:00 p.m. service by 5:40 p.m. and remain until the offering has been taken.
>
> It is of utmost importance that greeters notify me (665-4419) or Lucky Baldwin (668-6685), or the head usher in advance if for any reason you cannot greet. This will enable us to get a substitute; better still, it would be greatly appreciated if in your absence you get a substitute who is a member of the church.

Another form is headed: "The Ropes Go in Order As

Numbered," and is a diagram showing exactly which back rows should be roped off and in what sequence.

Still another form is headed: "Offering Plate Positions," and this too carries a diagram, showing usher positions when the offering is to be received.

All churches are concerned with attracting new ushers and maintaining their interest, though of course the smaller congregations have a more serious problem in this regard. Ideally, every usher on the staff should be alert to prospective ushers and see that names are given to the head usher.

Ideally, too, ushers should be especially identified in some way as they serve—whether by name badges or fresh flowers in the lapel. This serves several purposes: it provides immediate identification for members and guests; it lends dignity and uniformity to the proceedings, and it adds to a feeling of oneness and purpose on the part of the ushers themselves.

In their positions of leadership, head ushers must be careful not to show partiality or favoritism. The tendency or temptation might be to favor one's friends, and of course this is not right in the work of the church any more than it is elsewhere.

The church should see that its ushering staff is properly supplied: flashlights for possible emergency use; badges for identification, if needed; and an usher manual for each member of the staff.

Ideally, the head usher should submit regular reports to his supervisory person or board. Such accountability can only serve to help him in the performance of his duties, and of course it keeps the proper authorities informed of what is taking place on the ushering staff.

Even in the smaller churches, mimeographed assignment sheets—by the month or the quarter—not only help to keep the ushers informed but also lend credence to the importance of the responsibility. Too, they keep the pastor and other church leaders informed as to the people responsible for ushering during particular services.

Summary:

1. Be sure to have a head usher, no matter how small your ushering staff might be.

2. Have him responsible to some board of the church for purposes of reporting and accountability.

3. Maintain a list of active, reserve, and prospective ushers.

4. Have a job description for your ushers, in addition to specific written instructions each week for anything out of the ordinary.

5. Encourage on-the-job training by placing new ushers with someone more experienced.

6. Ushers on duty should be identified, either by a special badge or by fresh flowers in the lapel.

7. Head ushers must never show partiality or favoritism.

8. Keep the ushering staff properly supplied with flashlights, badges, usher manuals.

9. Prepare a mimeographed assignment sheet—by the month or quarter.

5

The Qualities of a Good Usher

One word—one quality or characteristic—stood out in our survey of church leaders as they faced the question of attributes that were especially important for ushers in the performance of their duties.

That word was friendly—but it was only one of literally dozens of qualities mentioned by these pastors and head ushers as they considered the behavior of these servants of the church.

Oscar McCullough of Chicago's famed Moody Church expressed it this way: "The church usher must be a friendly person concerned about helping others. Most of all, he must have a desire to serve the Lord and he must be faithful in his work."

In the view of Dr. Charles A. Epperson, the usher must be "present, prompt, personable, sensitive to the needs of others."

Lucky Baldwin and Carl Lofgren feel that the church usher should be a "godly man, friendly, outgoing, alert, neat and clean."

Rev. Stanley J. Lemon singles out friendliness, alertness to need, neat appearance, courtesy, gift of helps as vital characteristics of the capable church usher.

Emil Centanni, Lombard Bible Church, particularly wants ushers who are "dedicated—to the Lord, to their family, to the church."

Rev. Howard C. Stein looks for ushers who are "personally related to Christ, reflect His love; who are committed to and believe in their church; possess natural friendliness, warmth of personality, appreciation of people; and who must present themselves in an attractive and proper manner."

In the view of Ed Mark, these qualities are paramount: "Neatness, conservative dress—jackets, ties, well-groomed."

Rev. Ronald B. Gifford capsulizes his usher desires in three words: "Confident, friendly, faithful." As with some other churches, formal dress is not among the primary qualifications or prerequisitives for his ushers.

Dean Sonntag believes that the well-qualified church usher "does not behave in an offensive manner. He is extremely cautious in the handling of all kinds of people—friendly, polite."

Rev. Clarence E. Hager looks for "neat appearance—preferably suit and tie; friendly; cordial; available; informed; positive attitude; courteous; alert to areas of need."

Three major characteristics comprise the expectations of David Riemenschneider: "Neatly dressed, polite, friendly."

David Brandon adds a new consideration: "Friendly, smiling, observant, neat."

In the view of Rev. Donald A. Wiggins, the church usher should be friendly, relaxed, well-groomed, attentive, alert."

Ray Munsterman believes that "good ushers are easy to spot. They are friendly and helpful."

One might sum up these individual views of these leaders by saying they look for church ushers who are "friendly, neat, properly dressed, sensitive, willing to work, and spiritual."

Most church leaders look for Christian character in an usher before ability to serve and fulfill his duties. With that kind of background, the usher will naturally display the attributes suggested and desired.

Now let's consider some other desirable traits of the truly effective church usher:

Vision: "Where there is no vision, the people perish. . ." (Pro. 29:18), and without that same kind of vision a church usher might be able to perform his duties perfunctorily but not in a way that would honor and glorify the Lord. The good church usher should pray for a right vision of his duties before each performance of them:

> Dear Lord, help me to see my ushering job today as an opportunity to show forth Your love, Your joy, Your peace to everyone I serve. Make me an instrument in Your hand—to bless, and inspire, and cheer, and encourage.

Humility: ". . .In honour preferring one another" (Rom. 12:10). Some great saint of yesteryear declared that true humility is not necessarily thinking poorly of oneself, or well of oneself—but not thinking of oneself at all. A good church usher will be so occupied with proper care and concern for others that he will not be thinking about his own performance.

35

Dear Lord, help me to humble myself under Your mighty hand, so that I might truly prefer others before myself as I seek to serve You, Your church and Your children. Give me the heart and attitude of a servant—Your servant.

Calmness: "Thou wilt keep him in perfect peace, whose mind is stayed on thee. . ." (Isa. 26:3). In the midst of overflow crowds, with their crush and clamor, the church usher can remain calm and peaceful—not in his own strength, but by fixing his eyes and heart and mind on the Prince of Peace.

Dear Lord, keep me calm and sweet in the midst of any and every eventuality in the performance of my duties today. Help me to truly be Your spokesman in the moment of conflict or crisis, and to learn to be silent and listen—to You and to others. Help me to keep my words sweet, lest I have to eat them some day.

Flexibility: ". . .I have learned, in whatever state I am, therewith to be content" (Phil. 4:11). Learning to be adjustable to every situation, to unexpected changes, to sudden decisions, is a lifelong task, but one that the growing Christian continues to improve in throughout his lifetime. The good usher remains adaptable at all times.

Dear Lord, You know that normally I resist change and am often upset by sudden unexpected happenings. In my duties today, give me the

willingness—yea, Lord, the desire—to please
You by displaying a contented spirit that, in
turn, will foster contentment among all those
around me.

Reverent: "God is greatly to be feared in the assembly of
the saints, and to be had in reverence of all them that are
about him" (Ps. 89:7). Setting a proper atmosphere of
dignity and respect for the worship service is a prime
privilege and responsibility of the church usher. By his
attitude, bearing, and behavior throughout the service, the
usher is setting an example that can "make or break" the
true spirit of worship.

Dear Lord, keep me in awe of Your great power
and honor and glory as I seek to serve You today
in Your place of worship. Help me to be one who
leads the people, by example, to an attitude of
love and worship and reverence.

Punctual: "Redeeming the time. . ." (Eph. 5:16). More so
than with many other responsibilities, the church usher
must be on time for the performance of his duties, or they
will be totally neglected. Early arrivals at a worship
service, especially guests, must be warmly welcomed by a
caring usher. If the usher is not there to perform his duties
on time, the opportunity may be lost forever to affect the
life of a visitor for good.

Dear Lord, give me such a keen sense of priorities that I will never allow anything or anyone—

37

outside of genuine emergencies—to keep me from my appointed duties at the proper time. And if emergencies arise, may my concern for church responsibilities be so great that I will never neglect to obtain a replacement when circumstances prevent my being there.

Kind: "Be ye kind one to another. . ." (Eph. 4:32). The church usher must learn to act—rather than react—in the face of criticism or disfavor of any type, and that acting must be in kindness. That refers to fellow ushers as well as to worshippers who may be contacted only briefly.

Dear Lord, help me not to allow the petty grievances or behavior of others to set the pattern for my own conduct, but rather enable me by Your grace to show kindness—to everyone I contact, young or old, rich or poor, white or black. May the golden rule be operative in my life today: "All things whatsoever ye would that men should do to you, do ye even so to them. . ." (Matt. 7:12).

Submissive: "Obey them that have the rule over you, and submit yourselves. . ." (Heb. 13:17). The usher should heed the directions of the head usher without hesitation or question; similarly, the head usher is accountable to some authority over him, whether to the chairman of an official church board or to the pastor, or both. Submission to such authority is a sign of spiritual maturity.

Dear Lord, even as You became a servant and gave Yourself for mankind, help me to be a servant and submit myself to those who have been given responsibility for the ushering duties I must perform. May my submission to You be further evidenced by the manner in which I obey Your command to submit myself to those who have the rule over me.

Gracious: "Let your speech be always with grace..." (Col. 4:6). The grace of God—His unmerited favor to man—must be exemplified in one's dealings with his fellow human beings. A gracious spirit goes beyond mere smiles and outward condescension. The truly gracious person imparts a Christlike spirit that cannot be mistaken.

Dear Lord, even as You are the great giver of grace and mercy, help me to represent You worthily by demonstrating Your grace to those whose lives I touch today. May Your grace through me draw others to Yourself in a very real way.

Informed: The efficient church usher must know everything possible to know about his church and its leaders if he is to serve his constituency properly. This means extra effort on his part, but the resultant respect and good will created more than compensates for the time and effort required.

Dear Lord, as I try to represent You before

these people today, help me to be as concerned for their need of information and knowledge as You are. Help me to love them as You do, and thus have their foremost interests at heart.

Now let's give consideration to some of the qualities and characteristics suggested by church leaders who took part in the survey.

Friendly: "A friend loveth at all times. . ." (Prov. 17:17). Nothing is more heartwarming than to be greeted with a friendly smile, and the church usher has that opportunity many times during the performance of his duties. Great care must be exercised to employ a proper balance between genuine friendliness on the one hand and a proper attitude of dignity and reverence befitting the worship of Almighty God.

Dear Lord, help me to be a true friend—insofar as possible—to every person I serve today. May their color, age or status have no bearing on my recognition of them as friends. Help me to show a friendliness that many will want to reciprocate, realizing it comes from a heart warmed by your Spirit.

Clean (neat, well-dressed): Appearance is vitally important to the success of the church usher in accomplishing any of his goals as a servant of the people. And appearance covers several important areas: clothes, grooming, neatness. Exact mode of dress must be left to the good taste of the head usher and/or those in supervisory capacities over him, as they seek to convey to their faithful ushers something of the importance of appearance. The character (nature) of the church quite likely will determine the degree of formality required by its leaders for members of their ushering staff.

One church does not insist on suit and tie, yet worshippers seem just as fully capable of true worship as those where more uniformity and formality are required. Traditionally, most church ushers have appeared in full dress—suit and tie, but no one should say that any less of a worship experience is enjoyed by those fellowshipping in a church where more informal dress is permitted.

> Dear Lord, help me in my ushering duties to be
> so obviously involved in caring for others and
> their needs that appearance will not be a major
> concern of the worshippers. On the other hand,
> may I show proper respect for You and Your
> house by the way I dress. May my appearance in
> no way hinder any worshipper from
> experiencing true worship.

Sensitive, alert: "Bear ye one another's burdens..." (Gal. 6:2). Of utmost importance is the care and concern of the usher to be sensitive and alert to the needs of the people he serves. This means keeping a sharp eye for discomfort or discontent in any form on the part of worshippers.

> Dear Lord, if I'm truly exercising Your gift of
> caring for others, surely I will have an eye

41

constantly open to their needs. Give me a heart
like Thine, dear Lord, so that Your love will shine
through me to reach out to the needs that are
revealed to me. May I look after their comfort and
welfare in the same way You so bountifully look
after me.

Poised, relaxed: The church usher who truly sets the
right example for members of the congregation is the one
who remains poised and relaxed throughout the service,
regardless of developments and disturbances that might
otherwise disrupt the proceedings. This ability, too, is a
gift of God that must be prayed down in advance of its need,
though of course it is cultivated through the week by hiding
the Word of God in one's heart and spending time with Him
in prayer.

Dear Lord, as Your worshippers happen to
observe me through the service, may they see one
who is serenely carrying on his responsibilities
because of Your presence in his life and the
certain knowledge that You are in control. May
Your Presence in me draw them to You and to our
combined worship of You.

Faithful, dependable: Since the task of ushering is part of
the worship service, it is just as important for the usher to
faithfully carry on his task week after week, service after
service, as it is for the pastor and the Sunday school
teacher. Most pastors agree that dependability is one of the
truly choice qualities of the believer—especially one who

seeks to serve the Lord in the church.

Dear Lord, I want to be Your man in this job of
church ushering. Even as You remain constantly
faithful to me at all times and under all circumstances, may I be faithful and dependable in discharging my responsibilities to serve Your
church in the capacity of usher. May my sense of
priorities be so properly aligned with spiritual
values that I will never shun my duties for any
reason other than an emergency.

Available: May some prospective usher, looking for an
avenue of service in the church, prayerfully consider the
possibility of serving as church usher—an unsung and
unheralded task, but one with rich rewards to the faithful.
May they recognize the truth of the old saying, "God is not
looking for ability, but for availability."

Dear Lord, I want to be available for whatever
place of service You have in mind for me. Help me
to convey that same determination to my friends
and fellow members, so that they too might give
serious consideration to serving You by serving
Your church.

Dedicated, committed: As one head usher phrased it, the
church usher should be dedicated—committed—to the
Lord, to the church, to the church family. That makes it
easy to fall in line with all of the other qualities and
characteristics desired of the usher. If and when necessary,

that dedication should be renewed.

> Dear Lord, right now I dedicate myself anew to
> You for this important responsibility You've
> directed my way. Make such commitment so real
> to me that I will not be tempted to shirk my
> responsibility, but instead will rejoice in the
> opportunities You have made possible for me.

What efforts have pastors and head ushers made to cultivate these qualities among members of the ushering staff?

Rev. Donald A. Wiggins accomplishes that purpose "by
encouragement from the pastor and experienced ushers."

David Brandon seeks to cultivate these qualities among
his fellow ushers "by example."

In a similar vein, David Riemenschneider depends upon
"personal feedback."

Pastor Clarence E. Hager believes it can be accomplished
"by a careful, thoughtful head usher in his preparation."

"Prayer and love" are suggested by Emil Centanni as in-
centives for cultivation of these qualities.

"We try to guide the ushers," Ray Munsterman observed,
"but success really revolves around the personality of the
usher and his desire to do a good job."

Dr. Charles A. Epperson looks to "directives and
encouragement" for cultivation of these characteristics.

Lucky Baldwin and Carl Lofgren depend on "one-to-one
contacts and special meetings from time to time."

The best way, according to Rev. Stanley J. Lemon, is to
elect ushers who already possess these qualities.

Summary:

1.   Friendliness is a primary requisite for a good church usher.

2.   Other attributes: vision, humility, calmness, flexibility, reverence, punctuality, kindness, submissiveness, graciousness, informed, clean (neat, well-dressed), sensitive (alert), poised (relaxed), faithful (dependable), available, dedicated (committed).

3.   These qualities may be cultivated by: encouragement from the pastor and experienced ushers; example; personal feedback; prayer; love; directives; special meetings from time to time; elect ushers already possessing these qualities.

6

The Duties of the Usher: Greeting and Seating

Not every church considers their greeters part of the ushering staff. But in this manual we will assume that such is the case, since the majority of churches do combine those responsibilities of greeting and seating.

Because so many varied duties are included in the job description of the church usher, this chapter will deal only with the primary duties of the usher: greeting and seating. The next chapter will describe a number of specialized duties which can belong to the job.

Pastors and head ushers have responded to the question: "What are the duties of the usher?" For the most part, their responses will be carried in full within this chapter, even though the specialized functions will be dealt with in more detail in the concluding chapter.

Oscar McCullough, Moody Church, Chicago: "Ushering of people, passing out informational material concerned with the church, giving good directions in the church and in the area immediately outside of the church.

"The usher should be able to quiet down a person in a tactful manner if that person is disturbing the service. If he is not successful, then he should usher the disturber out as quietly as possible."

Dean Sonntag: "Control sound system, seat late-comers, collect offering."

Rev. Donald A. Wiggins: "Seat late-comers, distribute bulletins, welcome visitors, receive tithes and offerings, control lights and sound system, control thermostats and doors, handle phone calls during services, secure building, handle emergencies."

David Brandon: "Arrive at church ten minutes early; greet warmly while seating and handing out bulletins; be alert to where empty seats are; control heating, air conditioning, lighting; assist pastor."

Rev. Ronald B. Gifford: "Greet people, pass out literature, collect offerings, control temperature."

Dave Riemenschneider: "Greet people, pass out bulletins, seat late people, make the service go smoothly."

Rev. Clarence E. Hager: "First and foremost, to usher people to their seats with a bulletin for everyone. Recognize first-time visitors and give literature to each one. Seat late-comers. Receive the offering. Maintain the sanctuary and narthex for any emergencies and requests."

Emil Centanni: "Lighting, ventilation, save rear pews for late-comers, head count (sanctuary, cradle roll, nursery, children's church); have glass of cold water (in clean glass) available for use by pastor. See that visitor cards are given to pastor after service. Be at assigned stations fifteen minutes before service begins. Greet everyone—young and old. Usher everyone to their seats. When possible, ask people where they prefer to sit."

Rev. Howard C. Stein: "Ushers are responsible for the comfort of people in a church service. This includes their seating, physical comfort during the service, controlling sanctuary temperature, receiving of offerings, flow of traffic after a service and the various small items that fall upon one who is in essence the host of the hour.

"In a recent service, a man experienced a heart seizure. The ushers and church elders served very efficiently and kindly to the victim and his wife. An advantage was the presence of a medical doctor in the service. The service rendered by these persons, including ushers, continued until the ambulance arrived and the person was on the way to the hospital."

Ray Munsterman: "Greet people, assist them in finding Sunday school classes, take the offering, hand out bulletins, seat people, be helpful in any way possible."

Dr. Charles A. Epperson: "Care for any omissions in the readying of the meeting place. Greet, guide, provide assistance. Know where first aid equipment is; also, wheelchair."

Rev. Stanley J. Lemon: "Greet people on entrance into church; direct or lead them to a pew; distribute literature; receive the offering."

Lucky Baldwin and Carl Lofgren at Wheaton Bible Church have prepared a fourteen-point sheet of instructions entitled *Duties of an Usher*:

1. Report to head usher at least twenty minutes before start of service.

2. Should efficiently and mannerly escort all persons to their seats, especially visitors and strangers. If a person prefers a seat in the front, the usher at the rear should signal the usher up front to seat the person(s). Encourage the use of

the front seats prior to the beginning of the service.

3. Do not seat anyone during special musical numbers, choir, Scripture reading or prayer.

4. The two ushers in the two inside aisles stay together when taking the offering—even if this requires one to slow down or wait for the other.

5. *Always* face the rear of the church when taking the offering. *Do not look* at the people in the pews when waiting for the plate.

6. Always be alert and ready to render assistance to anyone needing it—be prepared to give aid in sudden illness—it's a good idea to keep a roving eye for such occurrences.

7. Know where the first aid kit and stretchers are stored and know how to operate the two types of stretchers. If you don't know where a doctor is seated in the sanctuary, make it your business to ask the head usher, so that the doctor's assistance can be quickly obtained should the need occur.

8. If a regular usher is unable to serve, he should notify the head usher in advance so a substitute can be contacted.

9. Help to locate visitors in the proper Sunday school class through the use of the information office in the Education Building.

10. Straighten hymnals and remove old bulletins and papers after the early service.

11. Maintain quietness in the foyer and

hallways and be alert for any disturbances.

12. Remove the ropes immediately after the service begins or as directed by the head ushers of that service.

13. See to it that there is proper ventilation.

14. Be happy to be in your work; above all, be courteous—remember whom you serve.

Some suggestions for performing the normal duties of a church usher may seem obvious, but perhaps they are worthy of this reminder.

No chewing of gum should be allowed on duty. Even when done discreetly, this practice is sometimes engaged in subconsciously and seldom is looked on with favor by other worshippers.

The use of some kind of mouthwash beforehand is strongly recommended. The person with bad breath usually is the last one to realize it.

When called upon by the pastor to hand out literature the usher should go immediately to the front of his area of responsibility and face the rear of the church. The worshippers will then be aware of the usher's presence and can indicate their desire for a visitors' packet or other literature.

Every usher should be fully aware of an advance plan of action in the event of an overflow crowd. That will enable the pastor and other church leaders to carry on the service smoothly despite what might be a distracting situation.

The church usher should not feel required to take the initiative in calling members by name as they are shown to their seats, nor should he feel the necessity of shaking hands with any on his own initiative. After the service, however, the usher should feel a responsibility to greet as many members and guests warmly and as personally as possible.

A conscientious usher will keep a small notebook, with pen or pencil, available at all times on duty, for the purpose of recording names of visitors. If nothing else, such a practice will help the usher in his efforts to remember names.

An usher should always make a special effort to straighten out any misunderstandings or hurt feelings resulting from actions taking place during the performance of his duties. For example, when a child disturbs the service and the usher notifies the parents that a nursery is available, some resentment might arise.

If there is even a possibility that such is the case, the usher should go out of his way to follow up—with a personal visit to the parents, if necessary—to smooth out any wrong feelings.

As suggested in an earlier chapter, it is helpful if ushers are easily identifiable—with an usher badge, a name badge or a fresh flower in the lapel. This, of course, is the responsibility of the head usher (or chairman of the ushering committee, as the case may be).

Seating people is an art in tact and diplomacy. In today's "liberated," more independent atmosphere, it is not always wise to attempt to coerce members and guests to sit in a particular section of your choosing, no matter how ideal it may seem to you and the pastor in the interest of worship. However, it is never wrong to suggest tactfully that a certain section is available if they so choose.

Some successful ushers find it helpful to ask the worshipper if he has any preference for seating. Others try to avoid this, lest the total seating arrangement fall into disarray and mar the service. Some people, of course, have become accustomed to a specific pew or section and normally will want to continue that custom.

Since an important part of the usher's duty is to make people comfortable, he will want to begin with a genuinely friendly attitude toward each member and guest. That friendliness must never become patronizing or over-solicitous.

As part of that balanced performance of his duties, the usher will always keep in mind the scriptural injunction, "And whatsoever ye do, do it heartily as unto the Lord..." (Col. 3:23a). Too, he will never forget the fact that all Christian service is accomplished by the Holy Spirit, which of course means that if your work for the Lord is to be truly Christian in its very nature, it must come from a heart, mind, and body that is controlled by the Holy Spirit.

That kind of service requires advance preparation, on a spiritual level—a deliberate and determined yieldedness to the control of the Holy Spirit for the performance of specific duties in the Name of the Lord. Ideally, that preparation will be part of the usher's quiet time throughout the week, culminating in special prayer preparation on Saturday night and Sunday morning.

Members and guests should be taken to their seats, never merely pointed toward them. And in the process of directing people to their seats, the usher must be careful not to walk too fast but let the worshippers set the pace.

If, as happens on occasion, the visitors or members do not

follow you all the way to the place you are leading them, you must simply walk back quietly to where they are seated and hand them a bulletin. This kind of slight embarrassment can be avoided by carefully watching their actions out of the corner of your eye as you proceed forward.

In the words of modern-day commerce, "the customer is always right." One pastor told of a guest brushing by an usher seeking to detain the people during a time of prayer, deliberately thwarting his intention and going to find a seat. Even in such instances as that, great care must be exercised to display Christlikeness in the performance of duties.

Such problems might be avoided, perhaps, by more carefully "sealing off" the entrance into the sanctuary at times when it is desired to maintain a worshipful atmosphere by keeping late-comers out until a song or hymn is sung.

The effective, Christlike usher will *act* (like a Christian) rather than *react* (to any discourtesy or rebuff on the part of worshippers).

In his role as a greeter, the usher should seek to learn the name of the visitor, then if at all possible introduce him to some member—who, in turn, might complete the circle of friendship by still another introduction or two.

Never yet has the charge been heard that a church is "too friendly." That, of course, means that it is impossible for your visitor to be greeted warmly by too many people. Ushers, more than any other workers in the church, are responsible for the friendly atmosphere—or lack of it—in the church.

Ushers should be alert to small children who leave the

service. Are they with an adult who has given them permission to leave? If not, do they need directions to a restroom, or supervision otherwise? Alertness to all movement in the service is strongly recommended.

As mentioned earlier, the head usher(s) should never show favoritism—to fellow ushers or to members and guests who happen to be personal friends. This might be a natural tendency, but it is one to be avoided. Lack of fairness is a fault that might be easily observable on the part of others, and thus distract from their attitude of worship.

Whenever a prominent person is present in the service, a note so stating should be conveyed to the pulpit for possible recognition. That does not mean, of course, that the pastor necessarily will welcome such a person specially, but at least it gives him the option. Perhaps the best time for giving such a note to the pastor is just as the offering is begun.

On the other hand, in the rare instance when a known "character" is in the audience—one who might possibly cause some distraction—the head ushers and fellow ushers should be quietly notified so they will be alerted to any possible disturbance.

People with hearing problems, if known to the usher, should be offered seats near the front of the sanctuary. If hearing aids are to be used, access to necessary outlets should be known in advance for the convenience of all concerned.

At least one usher should remain at or near the door during the service, so that disturbances and emergencies might be quickly discerned and handled.

On every trip up and down the aisle, the usher should be

scanning the pews for empty seats. This will facilitate his further efforts to find seats for late-comers.

In the instance where a small crowd is anticipated, two helpful steps can be taken: (1) lessen the size of the room, if possible, by dividers or screens; or when chairs are used, by thinning out the chairs; (2) by encouraging people to sit in specific areas that will help give the appearance of a more crowded room.

The alert usher will be prepared to offer his arm in assistance to an elderly or crippled person as they walk down the aisle.

While it is not a primary responsibility, still the church usher should keep an eye open to see that members and guests have hymnbooks available. Often it is possible for the usher to keep a hymnbook at hand—open to the appropriate selection—to present to the worshipper along with the bulletin as he is seated.

Look for evidence of physical discomfort—someone, perhaps, pulling a scarf or coat or shawl around the neck because of a draft, or someone fanning himself vigorously because of too much heat. Then make an effort to improve the temperature by proper controls.

By all means, keep a spiritual eye and ear open to the person who may be searching for an answer to his life, and be prepared to share something of the joy of knowing Christ with that person. It may be that you can arrange an appointment for such a visitor with the pastor, thus becoming an evangelistic arm of the church.

The usher should consider himself on duty throughout the service, and be prepared to see that late-comers receive a bulletin and are comfortably situated. At an appropriate time, usually just before the sermon, the usher should seat himself in his area of responsibility—yet still retain sensitivity to the needs of others in his area.

When the size of the church dictates, one set of ushers should be situated halfway down the aisle for the sake of convenience and facility in discharging their responsibilities. Signals may be set up between the two groups of ushers to facilitate the seating of the people.

Summary:

1. Major duties of most church ushers are greeting and seating.

2. Making the people comfortable is a chief responsibility.

3. The usher should arrive at least fifteen minutes early, preferably sooner, to be sure everything is in readiness and early arrivals are made comfortable.

4. Ushers should not chew gum, or in any other way call attention to themselves.

5. Avoid bad breath by advance use of mouthwash.

6. In handing out literature, proceed immediately to the very front of your area of responsibility so that worshippers might note your availability.

7. Know your advance plan of action in the event of an overflow crowd.

8. Keep a small notebook, and pen or pencil, at hand to jot down the names of visitors.

9. Always straighten out any misunderstandings that might arise in the performance of your duties.

10. Wear some kind of usher identification: usher

badge, name badge or fresh flower in the lapel.

11. Use tact: avoid coercion in the seating of people.

12. Prepare yourself throughout the week for your Sunday service for the Lord, by prayer and submission to God's Holy Spirit.

13. Remember, "the customer is always right." *Act* (in Christian love), never *react* (to discourtesy or rebuff).

14. Avoid favoritism or partiality—to fellow ushers and to parishioners.

15. Notify the pastor of the presence of a prominent person.

16. Anticipate a small crowd by (1) lessening the size of the room, if possible, or (2) seating people in comparatively scattered areas to give more of an appearance of a crowd.

17. Be alert for witnessing opportunities.

7

The Duties of the Usher:
Specialized Functions

In a very real sense, the effective church usher must be a jack-of-all-trades. While greeting and seating are his primary duties, still many other areas of responsibility might fall to him.

Many of these specialized functions have been referred to in the survey responses described in the previous chapter, but none of them have been discussed in detail.

In no particular order of importance, many of these extra-curricular activities will be discussed in this concluding chapter. It is not possible to cover every eventuality, for each church might have a different set of problems needing the attention of the usher.

One important assignment of the usher is the control of the temperature, and this is a matter needing constant surveillance. As the size of the crowd increases, of course, the temperature automatically rises, which means that someone must be prepared to turn down any heat or accelerate the air conditioning, depending upon the season of the year.

It is impossible to overstate the importance of this responsibility, for worshippers who are overly concerned with the temperature are neither comfortable nor attentive.

One thing must be recognized at the outset: it will never be possible to please everyone in a crowd of any size. But every conceivable effort must be made to please the members and guests.

Sometimes this means suggesting a possible relocation of the worshipper's seating place. Ideally, however, it simply means keeping a reasonably moderate temperature operative throughout the service. With the energy crisis, of course, and subsequent rules limiting the output of heating and air conditioning, the onus for discomfort can be passed on to the government and its mandatory restrictions.

Primarily, the usher must be sensitive to the people and make every effort to deal with the situation—either by actually making some change in the temperature or at least by satisfactorily explaining why nothing further can be done about the situation at that moment.

The great majority of people in any given crowd are sensible and understanding. To the small minority who may complain in such circumstances, the usher must simply keep his cool and try to explain his limitations in meeting the needs of everyone in the congregation. Most people will respond favorably to courteous and gracious gestures of cooperation.

A small but important responsibility is making a head count of the people in attendance—and this should include everyone in the building at the time of the count, whether in nursery, junior church or wherever. If the church has a balcony, this helps to facilitate such a count—for one can usually see and count more easily and unobtrusively from that vantage point.

If there is no balcony, each usher on the main floor might

have an area of responsibility insofar as the count is concerned. Such figures, of course, are then given to the head usher who in turn will come up with a total. The final count should then be given to the pastor or other delegated authority without fail.

Another concern of the effective church usher is the comfort and needs of the platform personnel. Are there sufficient chairs available? Hymnbooks? Is there a glass of water available for the pastor in the event of throat problems? Are the microphones in good order? Is everything in readiness for a smooth service of worship and praise to God?

That kind of responsibility does not end when the service begins, but must continue throughout the proceedings. In that way, no need or responsibility escapes the attention of the usher. The head usher, or person assigned by him, will see to these particular needs.

Likewise, the care and use of special equipment (overhead projectors, film and slide projectors, filmstrips, screens) should be the responsibility of one delegated individual. That usher, of course, should be one who is well-versed in the operation of such equipment and ready to meet any exigency that may arise.

When the use of such equipment is dictated, the responsible usher should check well in advance to be sure the necessary items are on hand, and operable. If the total care of such equipment is his responsibility, he should maintain a regular log in which anyone borrowing pieces of equipment checks out the item and again records its return. In that way, the delegated usher will know at all times where any given item is—and thus will never be at a loss at the last minute to come up with the necessary equipment.

Diligent attention to such matters as this relieve the hard-pressed pastor of important details that otherwise would require much of his valuable time. Insofar as possible, he should be kept free of such responsibilities.

Giving information is an important responsibility of every usher, and to be able to respond intelligently to all questions, he should keep himself well-informed on every aspect of church life. Ushers, in particular, should be regular readers of their own denominational publications, thus keeping apprised of the latest developments within their own group.

There will be times, of course, when an usher will not have the answer. Not only should he be willing to freely admit he doesn't know the answer, but he should also promise his questioner that he will make every effort to find the answer. And that should be done as quickly as possible, of course.

Well-informed ushers, who know Sunday school class and department locations, where the nursery and restrooms are, and many other similar items of information, help to create a good image for the church.

More needs to be said about caring for emergencies. Insofar as possible, any type of crisis that might arise should be anticipated and planned for well in advance. What would you do in the event of a person who faints; an unexpected outburst; a sudden intrusion upon the service? Depending upon their local situation and circumstances, each church might deal differently with such emergencies. The important thing is to have a plan of response for any and every crisis that might arise.

In some areas, it seems wise for one appointed usher to police the parking lot during the service, so that mischief and/or burglary might not take place. That usher might well be seated near the door, and absent himself every ten or fifteen minutes quietly to care for this responsibility.

That same usher, or another one specifically appointed, might want to police the entire church building during the service, for in more than one instance word has come of ladies' purses being stolen from the choir room while the service was in progress. An occasional tour of the building would insure that everything was in order.

Every usher should know the location of fire extinguishers, all exits, flashlights, candles and matches— in the event of fire or loss of electricity. If a fire alarm is inadvertently triggered in the building, every usher should know where to go to remedy the situation.

In many instances, it is important that at least one usher be on hand in the parking lot to assist in the flow of traffic. The head usher should be sensitive to this possible need and make provision for it if necessary.

As the "host of the hour"—or one of them—the good church usher should be sensitive to the needs of others the very moment he walks into the building. That means looking out for the sanctuary itself as to proper placement of hymnbooks, visitor registration cards, bulletins, and other such items. That means greeting early arrivals and making them feel at home, at the same time being alert to any who may have wandered in with spiritual or other needs.

One usher should be responsible for incoming telephone calls, and available to answer questions of parishioners as to the church policy regarding use of the phone.

In many churches, ushers often are pressed into service during the observance of Communion. This means, of course, that every usher should be familiar with the normal procedure followed during this ceremony, and available on call for such extra duty.

In the matter of registering guests, every church seems to follow a different pattern. But whatever system is used, the usher should be ready to assist before, during, and after the service, so that every visitor to the church is properly registered in one way or another.

Usher responsibility in many churches includes closing the church after services—putting everything back in order, replacing hymnals in the pew racks, gathering up bulletins left behind, putting away chairs, turning off heat and lights, closing doors and windows.

Summary:

1. Be alert and sensitive to every type of need.
2. Control the temperature of the sanctuary.
3. Help with the making of a thorough head count, as called upon by the head usher.
4. Attend to comfort and needs of platform personnel.
5. Familiarize yourself with the care and use of specialized equipment (overhead projectors, film and slide projectors, filmstrips, screens).
6. Be well-informed in order to answer the questions of members and guests.
7. Be prepared in advance for possible emergencies: fainting, unexpected outbursts, a sudden intrusion.

8. Police the parking lot at intervals during the service to prevent mischief and/or burglary.

9. Check the entire church building throughout the service, at regular intervals, to guard against thievery.

10. Know the location of fire extinguishers, flashlights, candles, matches.

11. Assist in the flow of traffic, if needed, in the parking lot after the service.

12. One usher should be responsible for incoming phone calls, and available to answer questions regarding church policy on use of the phone.

13. Be familiar with the proper procedure in the Communion observance in the event ushers are needed to assist in the distribution of the elements.

14. Do whatever is necessary and proper to assist in the registration of visitors.

15. Help close the church following services: replace hymnals in the pew racks; gather up bulletins left behind; put away chairs; turn off heat and lights; close doors and windows.